MAN ON A HORSE

MAN ON A HORSE
My Time with God in the Saddle

Mark Peterson

Artzaintsa
Books

Artzaintsa Books

www.Artzaintsa.com

PRINTED IN THE UNITED STATES OF AMERICA
17 16 15 14 13   1 2 3

ISBN 978-0-98984-830-5

All photography, unless otherwise noted, by the author
Cover design, interior artwork, and map: By the Stream Media www.bythestreammedia.com
Cover, contents page, and page 107 photography by Letitia Reasoner
Interior design: Artzaintsa Books

Publisher's Cataloging-in-Publication Data
Peterson, Mark.
  Man on a horse: my time with God in the saddle/Mark Peterson.
  ISBN 978-0-98984-830-5 (pbk)
  ISBN 978-0-98984-832-9 (ebk)
  1. Faith. 2. Travel—Religious aspects—Christianity. 3. Travel with horses—West (U.S.)
I. Title.
BV2450.2.P48 2013
248'.29 P48

                                                            2013949994

To Levi, Clay, Joy, and Jubilee

Contents

	Author's Note	ix
	Map of the Horse Trip	xi
1	Riding My Horse	13
2	Steer Wrestling	17
3	Leaving Home	21
4	Flooded	29
5	My First Week	33
6	In the Saddle	39
7	The Manna and Quail	47
8	Northern California	53
9	Snow	61
10	Men and Mountains	67
11	Horseshoes	73
12	In Oregon	83
13	Riding the Mule	89
14	Washington	93
15	Across the Border and Back Again	99

This is a true story. It is one I have told many times, and now, twenty years later, the time has come to put it in print. I wrote this book for my kids, Levi, Clay, Joy, and Jubilee in language that they can understand and relate to. For a deeper and more detailed version of the story, follow the footnotes, or rather "adult notes," at the bottom of each page. May it build the faith of many.

Enjoy.

Mark

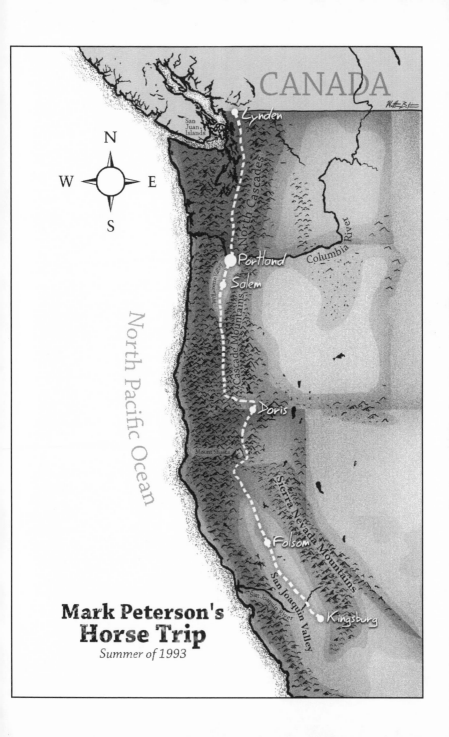

CANADA

Lynden

San Juan Islands

North Cascades

North Pacific Ocean

Portland

Salem

Columbia River

Willamette Valley

Cascade Mountains

Doris

Mount Shasta

Sierra Nevada Mountains

Folsom

San Joaquin River

San Joaquin Valley

Kingsburg

Mark Peterson's Horse Trip

Summer of 1993

Chapter 1

Riding My Horse

The day after I graduated from college I saddled up my horse and started riding north to the Canadian border. I ended up riding about fifteen hundred miles and it took me seventy days. That might sound like a good story right there, but what makes it really cool is that I did it without bringing any food or money. I never once asked for anything along the way, and I never missed one meal. This is the story of how it happened.

One day, I was looking out in the pasture at my horse and thought to myself that I should just jump on her and see how far I could go. I remembered that when I was little, my dad would take my brothers and me fishing up in the mountains every summer. We would ride our horses up into the Sierras and camp out up there for a week. One time my dad and brothers rode from our house clear to the ocean, camping along the way.[1] My mom and I drove out there with the horse trailer to pick them up once they'd made it. I was too little to go and wasn't too happy about being left behind.

With those thoughts running through my head, I started to think of all the places I could ride. My friend's family had a dairy up on the Canadian border and that sounded like the right place to go. Once I had the idea in my head, I couldn't get it out.

I had been wanting to do a big trip after college already, and up to that point, backpacking through Europe with a train pass, eating cheese had sounded really good. I'd even bought a bunch of books to help me do it. But the more I thought about it, the more I realized I wanted to see the country. Spending a few months in the saddle seemed like a better fit for me; the farm kid and cowboy in me wanted to ride.

One Sunday morning before church in early spring, I told a few friends that I was planning on riding my horse to Canada, and they all laughed at me. When the service let out that day, a lady walked up to me and a group of my friends while we were standing around talking.[2] She went to our church but I didn't know her very well. She looked me in the eye and said, "Mark, I

1. My dad and brothers rode from my hometown of Kingsburg, California to Cambria, California.

2. The woman who had the dream about me was Kim Crockett.

had a very specific dream about you last night. I wasn't even going to come to church today, but I did because I wanted to tell you the dream I had. In the dream, I saw you riding a horse north to Canada and God was using you powerfully along the way to tell people about him."

I was a little shocked and my friends weren't laughing at me anymore. We all started to get the feeling that this horse trip wasn't just my idea, but that God was in it. Later that day my friend Jon said, "Hey Mark, you should do the trip with no money or food—like when Jesus sent out the disciples."[3]

That really struck me because I had been reading a bunch of books about people who had trusted God to provide for them. The people from the stories in all those books never missed out on anything that they needed and they never had to ask for anything either.[4] I thought it over and decided, "If they can do it, I can do it too."

---

3. Jon Ward, a longtime friend. Luke 10:1–4 and Mark 6:8–10.

4. Some of these people include George Muller, Mother Teresa, Brother Andrew, Sadhu Sundar Singh, and Arthur Blessitt. I was also influenced by the book *A Walk Across America* by Peter Jenkins.

Chapter 2

Steer Wrestling

In a short time the horse trip, as it came to be known, went from a college graduation rite of passage to a full on Jesus Freak trip. If that was the way it was going to be, I wanted to make sure the whole thing was God. So I told him, "If this whole horse ride to Canada with no food or money, telling people about you is what you want me to do, then let me win the Laton Rodeo next Saturday and I will do it."[1]

The next week I was entered in the steer wrestling competition at the Laton Rodeo, a small town rodeo about fifteen miles from my hometown. It was Laton's biggest event of the year, and kind of a big deal in our

---

1. Judges 6:36–40. I was setting out a fleece for God.

area since it was the first of the spring rodeos. The weather in early April is about as perfect as California ever has, and the day of the rodeo was bright and sunny. The bleachers under the giant old oak tree were packed.

There were a bunch of really good, experienced cowboys there to compete. Most of them were guys I knew and had been practicing with, and I knew they were far better than I was. I had tried (not so successfully) in the past to ride bulls, but this was my first ever rodeo steer wrestling.

While I was waiting for my turn, I watched several other cowboys take their runs. Each one would line up his horse, wait for the chute man to open the gate, let the steer get a running head start, and then take off after it on horseback. When he caught it, he'd jump off his horse and wrestle the steer to the ground.[2] Most rodeo

---

2. Here's a fuller explanation of rodeo steer wrestling: The cowboy, sometimes called the bulldogger, starts out on horseback in the box. The steer is in a gated chute between the bulldogger and another cowboy on horseback, the hazer. The hazer rides alongside the steer to keep it running in a straight line when it's released. When the bulldogger is ready, he nods his head to the chute man, who then releases the steer. The steer gets a head start and pulls a rope barrier away from the bulldogger's box. When the barrier is released, the bulldogger can ride after the steer. He catches up to the running steer, leans over in the saddle, jumps off his horse to grab the steer by the horns, and wrestles it to the ground. When all the steer's legs are off the ground the clock stops. If the bulldogger breaks the barrier by taking off too soon, he gets a ten-second penalty added to his time.

events happen fast, but none of them are over as quickly as a good run for a steer wrestler, and these guys were turning out some pretty good times.

While I was waiting, one of the other cowboys came up to me to tell me about my steer.[3] He told me my steer had run in the slack the night before and that it had been matched up with a really good cowboy.[4] The steer ran that cowboy clear to the back of the arena, and he didn't even get a chance to jump. That cowboy took a no time, meaning he didn't even score at all. When I heard that, I knew that it would have to be God for me to win.

Before my turn came, I found my steer lined up to go in the chute, and when I thought no one was looking, I put my hands on it and started to pray. Just then, a guy I knew in high school who had been making fun of me for my faith the week before heard me praying and came up and laughed at me. I tried not to let it bother me and I felt a real peace that I was going to win.

It was my turn. With the help of some friends I got the horse lined up in the box and nodded my head to

---

3. Before the rodeo, officials match cowboys to steers in a drawing. Steers can weigh anywhere from 450 to 650 pounds and each one has a different temperament.

4. The slack is a spillover performance. It takes place prior to the main rodeo performance and gives cowboys who aren't slotted for the main event a chance to compete.

the chute man to signal that I was ready.[5] The gates opened up and it was all pretty much a blur. That steer went down fast, and the crowd went wild. I knew right then and there, before the times came in, that I had won and would be riding my horse to Canada. Even more importantly, God wanted me to do it.

---

5. The Hammerstrom brothers, Bill, Brad, and Brent, were the friends who helped me get ready in the box. I had practiced quite a bit at their ranch. Their father, Dennis, worked with me a lot and was a huge help to me. He was always telling me to "bow to the cattle," meaning to get in a bowing position on the steer's horns. Bill was hazing for me at the rodeo, and he said to me afterward, "When I saw all that hair flying around, I knew that steer was going down."

I bought the saddle that I took on the trip from Brad, who had won it in a rodeo. The saddle found its way back to him after the trip and is still in regular use at his ranch in Tracy, California.

Chapter 3

Leaving Home

Before I left I grew my hair and beard really long and prepared myself by not eating for a while.[1] I borrowed a pack mule because I knew I'd be spending some time in the mountains and figured I'd have a lot of supplies to carry with me. [2] I took the mule and my horse to a friend's ranch up in the mountains so they could get in good shape for the trip. I learned how to shoe a horse

---

1. I took the Nazirite vow, defined in Numbers 6, for nine months, and I also fasted for forty days. During the fast I lost forty pounds. My friends called me famine man.

2. I borrowed the mule from my older brother Aaron.

and tie a packsaddle with a diamond hitch.[3] I gathered up everything I could think of that I would need for the trip: my cowboy hat, some cooking stuff, my fishing pole, a tent, sleeping bag, knife, canteen, poncho, plus a little of this and a little of that—but no food and no money.

I had a lot of support from my friends, but some of them weren't sure what to make of my decision to go without provisions. Before I left, my friend Lynette tried to hide some money in my saddlebags but I found it and gave it back to her.[4] My pastor even thought I should bring some money with me in case of emergencies, but I told him I wasn't going to do it.

My life had changed a lot in the past few years because of meeting Jesus through friends at college, going to church with them, and inviting Jesus and his Holy Spirit into my life. I wasn't the same man anymore. Regularly, I would read things in the Bible in the morning and then similar things would happen to me and through me that day. I knew I believed that God was real, but there were still times I felt like I needed to know that he really cared about me, and that was part of the reason I decided to do the trip

---

3. My dad's best friend, Al King—Uncle Al to me—loaned me the packsaddle and showed me the diamond hitch. I learned to tie a double diamond hitch from a rancher along the way. I liked the double knot better as it held a more secure pack.

4. Lynette Casaretto, other than my wife, my best female friend ever.

like I did. Going out like Jesus's disciples had done, with no food or money, gave me no choice but to trust him for everything.[5]

Graduation day came and I did a short talk at the ceremony.[6] Then my mom had a party for me back at her house. My closest friends stayed behind after everyone else had gone home. Just before we were going to say good-bye, we all ended up standing with our arms around each other, like we were in a junior high football huddle, and we cried like babies together. It wasn't a sad cry, but one that we all knew was from the Lord because of what he was about to do.

I was pretty eager to start riding. There was a pull inside me wanting to go north like a migrating goose. The morning after my party, more friends and family

---

5. My main motivation for taking this horse trip wasn't just for the story or the adventure. I needed to know if God would do what he said he would do. Was he still the God of the Bible today, and not just yesterday? Would he meet me? Would it work? Would he provide? I wasn't sure, so I rode out to find out.

6. I was a communication major at Fresno State University. Our department had a separate graduation ceremony and each student had a few minutes to speak. I honored my favorite professor, George Diestel—I had taken every class he taught. I joked about how I had to buy a dictionary and look up twenty new words each day just so I could understand him. I gave him the dictionary in front of everyone during my talk and got a good laugh. George then walked up and gave the dictionary to the department head and got an even bigger laugh.

Saying good-bye to Todd and Donny

came to my house to say good-bye.[7] The last thing I did was make two stops, one at Jose's place and the other at Todd's to give them each a hug before I left.[8]

---

7. My cousin Brent, my mom, my sister-in-law Rosemary, and my friend Pete Grandle all came to say good-bye.

8. Jose Ramirez, a longtime employee, is one of my favorite people in the world. He knows how to get things done and have fun doing it. I am forever grateful for Jose. He is a great leader and is always finding a better way to do things. Many times when things were tough, he would say something along the lines of, "Mark, you can do this." Todd Bamford is a dairyman and my longtime friend. We've known each other since high school. You could always count on Todd for a good laugh and to say something encouraging.

And then, finally, I was leaving home.

When I rode off that day I felt really free, just me and my horse and the pack mule riding north through the fields. That afternoon I started to get a little hungry and thought I should stop somewhere and get the horses some water. I came up to a farmhouse and asked if I could water my horses. The farmer said, "Sure thing."

As I was talking to him about what I was doing, the horses were drinking and his wife came out and said, "I just made some beef jerky. Would you like some?"

I said, "Yes I would. That would be great." So she gave me a whole bag of jerky and a soda. I think that was the best beef jerky I have ever eaten.

I covered a little over twenty miles on that first day. It was easy riding over land that I knew well. That night as I was riding along the train tracks in downtown Clovis on my way to my friend Jim's place in Fresno, a lady walked up to me and asked me what I was doing. I stopped my horse, and after I told her she got tears in her eyes and offered to help me in any way she could. All I said was, "Thank you. I'm doing fine, but thanks." It was at that moment that I knew I was going to make it to Canada on the back of that horse.

I left my horse and the mule at Fresno State's rodeo corrals and stayed the night with Jim.[9] We went to church

---

9. Jim Drath, a.k.a. Jimmie Jack, and Jungle Jim to my kids, is a longtime good friend. At the time of the trip he had qualified to go to the Olympic trials as a pole-vaulter at Fresno State, and he was president of the Fellowship of Christian Athletes.

The top photo is of the first family to feed me on the trip. The one below was taken at the going away party with my friends from college and church.

together the next morning. Our pastor called me up front and told everyone that I was riding my horse to Canada with no food or money telling people about Jesus.[10] Then he invited anyone who wanted to, to come up and pray for me. It felt like the entire church came up, put their hands on me, and prayed.

That night my closest friends got together and had a spaghetti dinner. One of them brought his guitar and played a bunch of funny songs. We had a great time and I felt really loved. The next morning I left about half of my stuff at Jim's. After my first day I knew I was going to be okay and that I didn't need all that stuff anyway.

My horses were happy to see me when I went to get them in the morning.[11] I packed up, hugged my friends one last time, read a Bible verse, and rode off into the rising sun.[12] It was my only planned stop for fifteen hundred miles and now I knew I was on my own; excited and a little nervous, I rode out of Fresno headed north.

---

10. Mike Frye, my pastor and friend. I owe a lot to this man because he believed in me and loved me. I often ask myself, "What would Mike Frye do?"

11. I had gone to get some feed out of the dairy barn at Fresno State, but when I got back to the horses, someone had already fed them, and I knew God was telling me to trust him.

12. The verses I read were Philippians 4:11–13. I just flipped my Bible open to these verses and they were pretty telling of what happened the rest of the trip.

Chapter 4
Flooded

By midmorning I came to the San Joaquin River. It had rained a lot that year and the river was running at flood stage. I couldn't make it over the bridge on the road because there was too much traffic and my animals hadn't settled down yet. So I decided to put all my stuff in plastic bags and ride through the river.

I was doing great until just before we got to the far side of the river. The water got so deep that we all had to start swimming. I slipped off my horse, put one hand on the saddle horn, and paddled with the other. I didn't want to get tangled up with the mule so I let go of the lead rope. We only had about twenty feet more to go to get across and I figured she would follow me. Instead, she decided she'd had enough and turned around to go back. The current was too quick for her though, and she wound up getting pulled downstream. I watched her float farther and farther down the river until all I could see were two big ears and the packs, puffed up like a life jacket, go around a bend in the river. I'd lost her and all my stuff.

I turned the horse around and went back too, then rode downstream about a mile and caught her. I unloaded the packs, dumped out the water, retied them all, and tried crossing again. It was all super frustrating. This time I didn't let go when we got to the far side. We made it across, tired but happy.

That night I hung everything out to dry in an old riverbed. Nearly everything I'd brought had gotten wet and ruined except my father's camera; the plastic bag it was in was the only one that didn't leak.[1] No one had given me food all day so I ate field grain and oranges for dinner. I just picked the heads of wheat and rolled them in my hand to get the grain out. I tried to get some honey out of a dying beehive but the few bees that were left fought me off. I pitched my tent and built a fire. I hadn't even made it ten miles that day because of the river crossing, and I was exhausted. I crawled into my tent to go to bed and was sure that things would look better in the morning. In the middle of the night I woke up to the sound of rain, but I was happy and cozy in my tent and drifted back to sleep.

---

1. All but one of the photos included in this book were taken with my father's camera. I don't know how it wasn't ruined along with everything else that day.

My first night's camp set up in a dry
riverbed just north of Fresno

Something wet woke me up in the morning and I
looked around and realized I was sleeping in two inches
of water. It had rained so much in the night that the
river had started to run again and now everything that
had dried out from the river crossing the day before
was soaked again.

I loaded up my stuff after a breakfast of field grain
and rode off. I didn't get far though, because everything
was wet and the horses were not happy. Neither was I.
I was getting pretty discouraged when a man in a VW
Bug pulled up and asked me what I was doing. I said,
"I'm riding my horse to Canada and telling people about
Jesus." He told me he lived just up the road and invited
me to come over for lunch.

When I got to the VW guy's house, he treated me

like a king. He pulled off my saddles and oiled them, washed my clothes, and replaced some of the things that had been ruined by the river. I took a hot shower and he fed me a big roast beef lunch. Then, he just started talking about his life.

He said he knew God had sent me to him. We prayed and asked Jesus to help him get his life back together. Then, he pulled out a bunch of his drugs and threw them away right in front of me and started crying. He said I looked like Jesus and that he was so glad I had come, that it had changed his life and that he would never forget me. I was excited and felt God right down to my bones. He hugged me super tight and long before I left. It felt awesome to be in the right place at the right time with my heart in the right place, even if I had to have a few hard days to get there.

Chapter 5
My First Week

The next day I ate some leftover roast beef and then stayed the night in a barn in the foothills. Some cowboys were rounding up cattle so I helped them push a couple hundred head from one pasture to the next. I saw that one of them could ride really well and when we were done I learned that he had been a national champion cowboy.

My next stop was with some great folks who had a chicken ranch. They gave me a green Bible that I ended up using for the rest of the trip because mine had been ruined in the river.[1] I went to church with them in their

---

1. The Bible they gave me was a NIV New Testament only. It was a bummer that my Bible had been ruined, but in the end the change was good, because reading the simple language of the NIV and having only the New Testament got me right where I needed to be for this trip.

The chicken farmer who gave me my green Bible

old convertible with the top down and the wind in our hair. We got to their Bible study and they were studying Acts chapter 2, about the Holy Spirit. When we got there I thought for sure something crazy was going to happen, like doves flying in the window or something. There was a deep peace in the room that I could feel. Everyone there asked me a lot of questions about the Holy Spirit and I told them what I knew and had experienced since I had invited the Holy Spirit into my life.

A few days after that Bible study I was camping out in an almond field, and some field workers gave me some squash to eat. I tied up the horses and went to bed. The next morning I woke up to see the horse was all tangled up in her lead rope. I had left it too long, a major rookie mistake. Her back foot was rubbed raw

Roy Rogers's Friends

from the rope and super sore.

As she walked she was favoring that back foot pretty bad, so I ended up walking most of the day. Her foot kept getting worse and I started to sweat it because I thought that my trip might be over just as it was beginning; I was kicking myself and feeling pretty dumb for leaving her tied up like that all night. A defeated feeling was just starting to come over me when I came up to a nice, neatly kept farmhouse and asked the farmer where the best place to cross the river was.

As I was talking with him, his wife came out of the house, looked over the horse and pack mule, and asked me what I was doing. When I told her how far I was riding she looked concerned about the mare's back foot. Well, come to find out, she taught a horsemanship class at a college in Madera. She had every type of horse medicine imaginable in her barn and she took really good care of my horse.

They invited me to stay the weekend and offered me a bed in the house. I always felt weird when people I didn't know would invite me to stay in their house, so I just slept in the barn. They fed me really well. I worked on the farm on Saturday and then they took me around and showed me off to all their friends. I got to tell them about how cool God was, and pray for every one of them.[2] It was a lot of fun.

One cool thing about that couple is that they were friends with Roy Rogers, the first cowboy in the movies. They had pictures together with him all over their walls. Also, they were Catholic and had met the pope. Sunday morning I went with them to Mass and had a great time.

---

2. Shortly after coming to Christ, and on only my second visit to church, someone prayed for me and I had a good cry. I was wiping away the tears when the pastor, Mike Frye, came up to me and asked if I could help him pray for people. So I followed him around. He prayed, then I prayed. I didn't know what to pray so I just said what was on my mind and people cried too as they were touched by the Holy Spirit. I was hooked. Mike had helped open up a door for me to help others and bring them into contact with the living God. I followed Mike around for weeks after that and learned a lot. Then I just started praying for people on my own, with friends, in church and out, and with people I had just met. It was one thing to talk about God, it was quite another to invite him into the situation. I loved it so much, I would spend large portions of my day praying for everyone I ran into.

Riding the big yellow Harley

We stayed up talking late into the night. I felt really loved there.

Another cool thing happened that weekend. While I was at the barn, a biker pulled up on a big yellow Harley and asked me for directions. We started talking and he said, "You want to ride it?"

He hopped off, I got on, and there I went, riding down the road and across the river holding on to those big ape hangers and having a great time. Things like this happened to me the whole trip. I would mess up, like I did with my horse's foot, and God would turn it around and make it cool every time.

That Monday morning it was raining. I waited a few hours for the weather to break and then I was off again.

Roy Rogers's friends slipped me forty bucks just before I left and gave me big hugs with teary eyes.[3] It felt good.

About this time I wrote a letter to my church at home telling them about my first week out and all that God had done. My friend Lynette read it out loud at church on a Sunday morning. I heard it was pretty cool and made a bunch of people happy about my story so far because they were all praying for me back home.

---

3. That first money changed things. It was hard to take that forty dollars; I had to swallow some pride to receive it.

Chapter 6
In the Saddle

Life is different on a horse. For the most part you're just checking things out, going three or four miles an hour while the rest of the world is going seventy. When you're walking, you're watching where your feet are going, but on a horse you're looking at everything, taking it all in. It's the best way to see the country.

A lot of people asked me how I planned to ride to Canada. They wanted to know if I would use the Pacific Crest Trail, or how I would know which way to go.[1]

I did ride the Pacific Crest Trail some of the time, but for the most part I rode through farm country,

---

1. The Pacific Crest Trail is a twenty-six hundred mile hiking and equestrian trail that runs from California's border with Mexico to the border of Washington and Canada.

because there weren't as many fences and it made me feel more at home. Sometimes I rode along ditch banks, logging roads, railroad tracks, fence lines—anything that would get me north in a straight line. I had a road map, but for the most part I just kept riding north. I didn't have a compass, but I do have a pretty good sense of direction and a lot of times I used the sun to know which way to go. On cloudy days I just guessed and got a little off course sometimes, but when I did, I would always meet some really great people and have the chance to talk to them about God.

Seems like I ended up spending the night in the craziest places. About an hour before dark I'd start looking for a good spot to camp, and if I could get permission to stay, I would. I'd pull off my horse's saddle, take the packs off the mule, pitch my tent, roll out my sleeping bag, build a fire, and eat whatever food I had with me. After the horse hurt her foot, I'd just tie her by one of her front hooves at night. I didn't need to tie the mule because she would stay right by the horse's side through the whole night and wouldn't run off. They were best friends and wouldn't leave each other.

For the most part I slept really well because I was so tired from riding all day. In the first section of California, the more wild places were corners of farmers' fields or dry riverbeds. In the mountain sections of the ride, I camped out along the trail, and in Oregon and Washington I spent most nights in farmers' hay barns. I'd roll out my sleeping bag on top of the hay and spend the night with the barn owls. They'd hiss and screech at me,

How I spent most of my nights in hay barns

but I was always so exhausted from riding that I would be asleep the second I laid my head down, so I didn't mind. Sundays would roll around and I would rest up and be ready to hit the road again on Monday morning.

Sometimes people would invite me in. When I would stay with people, we would talk late into the night about life and God. I would pray for people and give them the best of me.

I became really connected to the horses over all those miles. Most of the time I wouldn't even tie them up when we would take breaks. I'd just take the horse's bridle off and let her graze while I would nap in the

I had plenty of time to joke around. Both of these pictures were taken somewhere in Oregon.

grass or read my Bible. Even so, the horse and mule would run off and leave me sometimes if they got spooked. There was usually someone around to help me catch them.

While I was riding, I sang every song I could think of. I prayed a lot and worshiped God a lot. I would just sing the same songs over and over.[2] I could feel the whole trip that I was under God's mercy and I was trying to pull on it, keep it right there with me. A lot of the time I just thought; I had time in the saddle to think about everything.

I got used to people pointing and looking at me. When I was riding along roadways, people in cars and trucks would pull over way ahead on the side of the road and wait for me to ride up. I'd talk to them and pray for them. Sometimes people wanted to take a picture with me. My beard had gotten pretty scraggly and most of the time I was dirty and looked road-weary, but after a while, how I looked to other people didn't bother me very much.

The whole trip I gave kids rides on the horses. No matter where I was, the kids acted just the same, they

---

2. The song I sang the most was "I Lift My Eyes Up (Psalm 121)." It fit the trip. It expressed my need, God's greatness, and the beauty of creation. Plus it has a melody and is in a key I can really belt out nice and loud. I would sing it over and over. Sometimes a song is not just worship but a prayer, allowing you to sing things you would never be able to say. I felt close to God when I was singing it.

Giving kids rides along the way

loved it. They'd just get giddy and excited about the chance to sit on the back of the horse. Sometimes the kids wanted to wear my hat too. A few of them were shy, but you could see in their eyes that this was a big deal so I never rushed when talking to kids or giving them rides. One little girl that I met in a park in Northern California told me she thought I should call my horse Happy Meal, so from then on, I did.

Chapter 7

The Manna and Quail

I never missed a meal the whole trip.

Sometimes all I had was oatmeal and rice. And sometimes I got pretty tired of it. A couple weeks into the trip, I was out in the middle of nowhere, miles from a store and I was all out of meat. I'd already had a few days of eating only oatmeal and rice and I started to complain to God about it. I felt like eating pizza and Mexican food, but I only had oatmeal and rice. In the midst of all that complaining I thought of the manna and quail story in the Bible and became thankful for what I had.[1]

That night as it was starting to get dark, I made camp by a river. I didn't have time to fish, but I went down

1. Exodus 16.

to the river to get some water to cook my rice. While I was dipping my pot in the water, a fisherman in a float tube was drifting toward me on my side of the river. When he reached me he stopped and asked what I was doing, and I said, "Riding my horse to Canada and telling people about Jesus."

We kept talking and he started cleaning all the fish he'd caught that day. They were big fat river bass. When he was done, he held them up and said, "That's a good thing you're doing. You want some of these fish?" I said, "Sure." He handed all of them to me and then just kept on floating downstream.

When I got back to the fire, the coals had burned down so I grabbed some foil and cooked the fish over the coals. Man, those were the best fish I have ever eaten in my life. It was just like eating the manna and quail. Looking back, that man never told me his name and I think that maybe he was an angel.

That fish story was pretty telling of the rest of the trip. Whatever I got hungry for was exactly what people would feed me. One time I got to craving Chinese food and sure enough, some folks at a church in Folsom took me out to a Chinese restaurant. Another time I wanted hamburgers and fries and a man pulled over and offered to buy me lunch right as I was passing this great little roadside hamburger stand.

My favorite story along this line is what happened the week of my birthday. I was staying at a cowboy's ranch that week; that guy was a real horseman. He showed me the double diamond hitch for the pack mule, and how to tether my horse by the foot so she wouldn't get tangled up or hurt again. And, he had a Chris LeDoux tape that I was really happy to hear.[2]

The rancher's wife served up a great dinner. It was awesome. After dinner, she went into the kitchen to bring out dessert. When she came around the corner, I saw that she was carrying a layered chocolate pudding cake. It was the same exact dessert that I would ask my mom to make for me every year on my birthday. The rancher's wife had no idea. It was a beautiful God-loves-me moment. The next morning when I left, the rancher saddled up and rode out with me for a few miles. It made me feel strong to ride with a real cowboy for a while.

Another time, when I was in Oregon, I had gone up in the mountains out in the middle of nowhere and I was completely out of food and money. I was getting a little hungry and considering my circumstances. I thought, "Well, I don't know how you're going to feed me this time God." Just as I was thinking that, a man

---

2. I bought my first Chris LeDoux tape over the feed store counter when I was eighteen and have been listening to him ever since. I was in his fan club for years and went to a bunch of his concerts. Though I never met him, he was a father to me. When I found out Chris died in 2005, I cried for two weeks. I took a thirty-six hour road trip down to Cheyenne, Wyoming, picked up my friend Neil, a rancher out in Bozeman, Montana, and went to hear Toby Keith do Chris's memorial concert. We stopped in Chris's hometown, Kaycee, Wyoming, population 255, on the way and left a homemade tribute to him at the rodeo grounds.

The rancher whose wife unknowingly served me my favorite birthday cake the week of my birthday

came walking up out of the middle of the woods. He looked like a logger and had on loose-fitting pants with the bottom hem cut off, held up by suspenders. I don't know how he got there, but all of the sudden he just showed up and asked me what I was doing. When I told him, he said, "My wife packed me way too many pork chops for lunch today. Would you like some?"

Later, I sat on a log and ate those pork chops smothered in barbecue sauce with my hands, straight out of the plastic bag they were packed in. It was a really happy moment for me; I had a good laugh because God did it again.

The kid who gave my horses a ripped bag of grain

And it wasn't just me, the horses had to eat too. Over and over again people helped the horses as much as they helped me. New rope, saddle blankets, medicine, whatever they needed it was there all the time. I can't tell you how many times I would tie up my horses and come back to see that someone had already fed them or given them water.

On the day of my birthday, I had gone into a bar to have a lemonade and when I came back to the horses, a guy from the local feed store had given them a ripped bag of grain. He had on dark sunglasses and when he handed the grain to me, a big tear ran down his face. It embarrassed him and he tried not to let it show, but

I saw it. That kid didn't know what was going on but I did. God had moved his heart to help me and he was being blessed just as much as I was. Later that same day I found another bag of grain on the side of the road. Riding off that day, I had way more grain than I needed or could carry.

Chapter 8

Northern California

I was traveling light, and getting lighter everyday as my trust that God would provide for me grew. It felt really good and freeing not to be burdened by carrying a bunch of stuff. And, my horse was doing great, thanks to the help from Roy Rogers's friends. Since I had a little money, I bought some food and I was eating good regularly. Plus, I had been riding through farm country in the middle of summer so there was food everywhere—fruit, nuts, berries, vegetables, and my favorite, cherries.

As I rode out of the San Joaquin Valley, the fruit and nut trees disappeared and I ended up riding through some of the richer areas around Sacramento. I saw all those big houses and yards filled with boats, motorcycles, and nice cars with no one around to enjoy them, and I thought to myself, "What a waste." God started

Eating cherries

speaking to me about possessions and I made a lot of decisions during that trip that I still live out of today.[1]

When I rode into Folsom I decided to stay at the

---

1. All those big houses were full of expensive things, but at the same time totally empty because the owners were out working so they could make the payments on all that stuff; they didn't even have time to enjoy it. When I saw that, I knew I didn't want to live that way. I was spending hours a day in the New Testament, reading verses like Luke 14:33: "...those of you who do not give up everything you have cannot be my disciples." Something stirred in me when I read that scripture and others like it that I couldn't ignore. Those verses demanded action. So when I got home months later, I sold or gave away everything I owned. Even though I was only twenty-five years old, I'd been working since I was nine and I had a bunch of stuff. It took about a year to unload everything. My guns were the hardest thing to see go;

rodeo grounds in the announcer's booth. I was there the weekend of the Folsom Rodeo and I let the horses feed on leftover hay. Being around a rodeo always made me feel free. It was Sunday, a day I promised myself I wouldn't ride. So, I cleaned up as best as I could and found a church to go to. The pastor at the Folsom church called me out to give a testimony, so I did. The people there took me out to lunch, bought me supplies, fed my horses, and then took me home for dinner.

The next morning when I woke up in the announcer's booth, the whole rodeo arena was full of prisoners

---

I had a nice collection. It was hard but I was confident in the decision. It was something I knew I needed to do. Stuff had a hold on me that needed to be broken.

For years, I didn't think much about it and was really happy. I traveled the world, lived off just a little, and didn't own much to speak of. It was great to be out from under the responsibility and blown about by the wind. But a few years after I got married, I started getting tired of being broke. Regret about selling my stuff, my land, and my houses would creep in and stay for a while before I could shake it off. I was comforted by Saint Anthony, who sold his stuff and went into the desert to find God only to be tempted for twenty years by regret. He overcame it and great things happened. Now, twenty years later, I can say the same. The move to sell everything, for me, made and continues to make it easier to keep eternity in mind. The stuff lost its power. And today, when I buy something I make sure that I use it regularly; if I don't, I get rid of it. I make sure that I own it, and it doesn't own me. I prefer to spend the money that we do have on experiences for our family, instead of stuff. I live simply because of what I learned on this ride and I am thankful for those lessons, especially that God will provide for me.

Sleeping in the announcer's booth at
the Folsom Rodeo Grounds

cleaning the place up. I could see Folsom Prison just a
little ways away. The scene really struck me and I wrote
a poem about my whole weekend.[2]

On my way north, I saw California's rice fields for
the first time in my life. They were bright green and
pretty hard to ride through because at that time of year
the farmers were irrigating and the fields and ditches

---

2. I could see Folsom Prison from the rodeo grounds and it
made me sad, and then hungry to spread the freedom message
I was living in. I couldn't express it all fully, so I wrote a poem
and felt a real peace after getting my thoughts and feelings on
paper. Unfortunately, the poem was lost years later along with
my journal.

were full of water.

When I rode into Redding, I bought a bunch of food and headed up the Pacific Crest Trail. The year I was riding it had snowed a lot more than usual. Once I was on the trail I hit snow right away, but it was patchy so I just kept going.[3]

When I started out on the trail I saw a huge rattle-snake. I thought about killing it but I just left it alone. About a half day into the ride, I was up in the Cascade Mountains and it was beautiful. The smell of ponderosa pine hung in the air. The rock formations set against the blue sky were pretty amazing, and there were wildflowers everywhere. It felt good to finally get out of the valley and into the mountains.

Toward the end of my first day riding in the Cascades, I came to a section of trail that ran along a high shale ridge. It was pretty narrow and my horses had to walk in single file, one right after the other. One side of the trail dropped off down a steep rocky slope of crumbled shale into a boulder field about five hundred feet below. There was a little snow up on top of the ridgeline and I remember seeing a huge buzzard, or maybe it was an eagle, flying around right about level with me. I started feeling pretty cool and happy with myself, like I was the Marlboro Man. Just when I started thinking that, I heard a noise behind me and turned around to see the

3. The snowpack in the Sierras in 1993 was one of the highest recorded in my lifetime, at the time of the trip.

Riding out of Burney, California to start on the Pacific Crest Trail

mule slipping on a loose piece of shale rock. Her front leg buckled and in an instant she started slipping down the steep slope.[4] She did a full 360 degree roll and I just let go of the lead rope; I knew she was as good as dead and headed straight down to the boulder field, and I didn't want to go with her.

Then a miracle happened. There was a scrappy spruce tree growing out of the side of the cliff just beneath the place on the trail where the mule lost her footing.

---

4. This was the only time the mule slipped the entire trip. She was one of the most sure-footed animals I have ever seen.

Crossing a bridge on the Pacific Crest Trail

It was just about six feet tall, and bent by the wind into the form of a hook. The mule's fall landed her right square perfect on that tree and the hook caught her in the belly. It bent way back beneath her weight and then catapulted her onto the trail behind me, only now she was facing the opposite direction.

I saw the whole thing and I couldn't believe my eyes.

I lost a few pots and pans when they came out of the pack and bounced clear to the bottom of the boulder field, as if to make the point that the mule would have done the same thing if that tree hadn't been there. Since the mule was now facing down the trail, I just went up a bit until I had space to turn around and then went back down the trail to get her. I had a bewildered, humble, I'm-really-lucky feeling that made me grateful.

Chapter 9

Snow

I fought through the snow for days after that, regularly crossing snowdrifts that were as high as twenty feet. There were downed trees across the trail left and right, so I ended up doing a lot of cross-country riding.[1] The biggest problem with the snow was the lack of feed for the horses. I knew they weren't getting enough, so I

---

1. A month or so before I left on my trip, I got the chance to talk with a guy who'd ridden the entire Pacific Crest Trail on horseback the year before. He said there was only one bad section on the trail, where trees were down all over and the riding was near impossible. I didn't remember that conversation until I was already up in the mountains and riding the very same section of trail he had told me about. It was the only section of the PCT I rode the whole trip.

would stop at every patch of grass I saw and let them eat it down.

After one night spent sleeping in the snow and another blocked in on the trail with no way to get water, I rode into a beautiful meadow. I'm not sure why it wasn't full of snow too. It was like an oasis, right up on top of those mountains. I took a long drink from a crystal-clear creek, made camp, and turned the horses loose in the meadow. Man, were they happy, and so was I.

The next morning was a Sunday, my rest day, and I awoke in that beautiful meadow. It was the perfect place, all green and pretty and surrounded by snow-covered mountains. I made a corral for the horses out of tree limbs so they could graze freely at night instead of being tied up. After so many days of hard riding, I was finally able to just rest and relax in the beauty of the mountains.

But then something began to happen. As I told you before, my dad used to take us up in the mountains every year on horseback, so being in that meadow made me have a lot of memories. The sights and the smells made me really start to miss my dad and I couldn't stop thinking about him off and on all day. Later in the afternoon, I walked out to the middle of the meadow and sat down on a log. I was just sitting there thinking and I began to get real sad. I got so sad that I started to cry because I was missing my dad.[2]

2. It was early to mid-June when I rode into the meadow in the Cascades, the same time of year that my brothers and I would take our annual horse trips with Dad. I didn't make that connection until twenty years later, while writing this book.

1. The Pacific Crest Trail blocked by snow
2. My camp on the trail when I was blocked in by downed trees 3. The first stream I found after two days trapped on the trail

One thing you should know is that I never cried when my dad died. Not once. It didn't mean that I didn't miss him, or that I wasn't sad. It's just that I was never able to cry. So there I was in the mountains, fifteen years later, and I started to cry over it for the first time.

I cried, then I cried some more. I couldn't stop. I cried so long and so hard that I started to lose my voice. I was up in the middle of nowhere and I didn't really care because there was no one to hear me, so I just kept crying.[3]

Then something crazy happened. I had my eyes closed, but I saw my dad walking across the meadow. He walked right up to me and sat down on the log beside me, put his arms around me, and sat there for a while; and I just cried. Then he looked me in the eye and said, "Son, I love you, and I'm real proud of you."[4]

Hearing him say that made me cry more and I just couldn't stop. He just sat there with me for a while. Then he stood up and walked back across the meadow. I didn't want him to go so I tried to call after him but I

---

3. I went to several counselors for help in my early twenties and they told me that I needed to grieve the death of my father because I never had. They gave me exercises to do, like to write him letters and go to the grave and read them out loud, but nothing ever worked.

4. I knew growing up that I was loved and that my dad was proud of me, but I never remember him saying it until then.

couldn't. I wanted to follow him so I tried and tried to open my eyes but I couldn't get them to open. It was all so real. It felt like I could just get up and go with him, but I couldn't move.

When I was finally able to open my eyes, my dad was gone. I just sat on that log for a long time and my heart felt so much better. I missed my dad, but he had come to say hi, and he'd told me what I really needed to hear.

Chapter 10

Men and Mountains

So many people encouraged me along the way. It happened a lot that one person I'd met would tell a friend in the next town that I was going to be riding through, and then that friend would drive around until he or she found me, and take care of me too.

Every time I started to get hungry, I figured I was about to meet someone, so I'd get prayed up and prepared to meet the next person. It became a pattern that I could trust; that person was going to feed me and I was going to feed them.[1]

I would usually meet people one of two ways: by

---

1. The trip just wouldn't have worked without all the people that fed me and took care of me; the whole thing is a testimony to the fact that we need community and that God made us a body.

asking if I could water the horses or camp on their property, or by someone coming up and asking me what I was doing. I could tell within the first sentence of the conversation whether God was on it, and whether something was about to happen.

The first few weeks of the trip I was in survival mode, still testing the waters and seeing how this whole thing was going to pan out. But by the time I made it to far Northern California, I knew I was going to make it. At that point, I started focusing more on what God was doing in the lives of the people I met. When people asked me what I was doing, I'd answer by saying that I was riding my horse to Canada telling people about Jesus, and I saw the power of his name. I noticed that the second I would say "Jesus," it was like the person I was talking to had been hit over the head with a two-by-four. I kept seeing it happen. All different kinds of people would just start tearing up, and become really open with me—maybe sometimes without even knowing why. Time and time again, God's power to touch people's hearts was carried in on the name of Jesus. I kept seeing it happen, so I kept saying it.[2]

---

2. Seeing the way the name of Jesus affected people that I talked to on the trip had a big effect on me. I learned that the name of Jesus is a dividing line, it defines our faith. It has power and lets others know where you stand. It shifts atmospheres. It's the part of the Trinity that regular people understand and love. I saw that he is inside of us and when we say his name it changes the lives of those around us.

The woman who washed my clothes by hand

One time a man walked right up to me when I was on my horse, looked me in the eyes, put his hand on my leg, and just started crying. He never said anything and then just walked off crying. I didn't know why he did it. Moments like that made me think about how big God is, and what he was doing in people's lives that I didn't understand or need to. It made the everyday happenings on the trip feel eternal. There was a peaceful respect for God's presence inside me, and I just felt honored and grateful that he was using me in this way.

People gave me several books along the way. My

The man in the top photo was a colonel in the army. The man in the photo below helped me out when I was in the mountains in Oregon.

favorite was *Of Men and Mountains*.[3] I read the whole thing and loved it. But mostly I read my Bible.

People I would meet were always wanting me to stay longer, or to go visit this friend or that one. A lot of people wanted me to come on a radio show or do an interview for their newspaper, but I turned all the offers down. I felt like the horse trip was between me and God and that I would talk about it when I was ready.

Sometimes so many people would stop to talk to me that I would get really tired and just want to get back to riding again. When I got like that I would ride up in the mountains to get away from people and camp out.

---

3. By William O. Douglas. I loved it because I connected to his time in the wilderness and it made me feel understood.

Chapter 11

Horseshoes

When I came down off the Pacific Crest Trail, I camped along the McCloud River. I was out of meat and broke out my fishing pole to catch some dinner. I have done a lot of fishing in my life, but fishing is a whole different thing when you're hungry and you don't just want to catch fish, you need to catch fish. After I caught a few, I cooked them on the fire and man, were they good. When I was finished eating, two local women who were out on a day ride nearby brought over some hay and grain to take care of the horses. It made the horses really happy.

From there I rode into a little mom-and-pop town at the base of Mount Shasta. A shopkeeper invited me to come over for dinner. The food was good, but her

The women riders who brought my
horses feed at the McCloud River

house was a little weird and she believed in a bunch of
weird stuff; when she started talking funny I got the
creeps, so I got out of there.[1]

---

1. I debated whether I should include this note, but this was a
spiritual trip and what happened here was an important spiritual
event; it belongs in the story. Ephesians 6:12.
The woman who invited me for dinner owned a new age shop in
town. The first strange thing I noticed at her house was the empty
box of fruit from my family's farm sitting on her front porch. She
had a black crow in the house, several black cats, and a black stud
horse in the barn. I noticed the crystals and several other occult
items scattered throughout the house, but I was exhausted after all
those long hard days in the mountains, and I was looking forward
to a good meal and a bath. She served a nice dinner and invited a
friend to join us. Most of the conversation was light, but toward
the end of the meal the women asked me why I was taking the
horse trip. When I said the name of Jesus, my host became very
uncomfortable and there was a distinct change in her face. She

I left town and rode a lonely old logging road called Military Road that went all the way around Mount Shasta. I only saw two cars during the three days I was riding that road.

When I came out on the other side of the mountain, I stayed with a great bunch of forestry workers in a cabin that an early rancher had built. It was over a hundred

---

asked me if I believed in healing and I said yes. She said I'd hurt my back and that she could heal me. Then without asking my permission, she touched my back and I felt a dark presence come on me. I quickly stood up, told her I had not hurt my back, and that it is Jesus who heals. I thanked them for dinner, walked out of the house, left my horses in the barn, and walked/ran into town to call my pastor from home. It was one of two times I called anyone the whole trip. I was pretty freaked out and I needed prayer. Mike prayed for me and so did his wife, Betty. After that I felt a lot better, but a violated feeling was still stuck in my gut. I would have ridden out that night but it was pitch black outside, so I slept in the barn. I hadn't had any trouble sleeping the entire trip, but I was in and out of sleep all that night. The cats were meowing in my ear and the stud horse was stomping its feet and making noises. I would wake up and pray, and then fall back to sleep. In the middle of the night, I had a vivid nightmare that demons were trying to take my spirit out of my body and carry me away. I was trying to say the name of Jesus, but I couldn't speak. I was struggling and struggling. In the dream I was up in the air, looking down on my sleeping body in the hay. I finally got out the words, "Jesus help me." At that instant I woke up. I was shaken, and I started to pray like I had never prayed before. At first light I was saddled, packed, and out the door. My host's friend met me at the gate and apologized profusely for the whole incident. I was rocked, still filthy, and exhausted as I rode out toward Mount Shasta. Days later, after tons of prayer, I started to feel calm again.

Snow-covered Mount Shasta

years old and sat on the edge of the pines, overlooking
a big meadow with rail corrals for the horses. I took a
Sunday off there, ate great, had a few laughs, and took
the first shower I'd had in a long time.

When I was on my way through ranch country in far
Northern California, a man in a truck pulled over on the
side of the road to wait for me. He seemed to know who
I was and surprised me by calling me by name as he gave
the horses some grain. It turns out, he knew the ladies
who brought my horses hay and grain in McCloud. It
was always a little weird to get called by name by people
I didn't know, but when I figured out how they knew
me, it would always make me happy.

I crossed the Oregon border in Doris, California.
Crossing the state line was a relief because it felt like I
had been riding in California forever. I set my sights on

The hundred-year-old ranch cabin with great
corrals and Forestry workers saying hi to the horses

the Willamette Valley and headed northwest. As I was riding through the mountains I came upon a little old cabin with some horses in a corral out back. I started talking to the old guy who lived there and he invited me to stay. He didn't have a bathroom or running water, but he did have electricity. He was a pretty rough guy in general and seemed pretty lonely up there all by himself. I never could tell exactly what he did for a living.

After breakfast the next morning he asked me if I knew how to put shoes on horses. I said, "Yes I do, and I have all the tools with me except an anvil."

He said, "I have an anvil and the shoes if you can put them on."

So I went to work. He had two young horses that he wanted done and after working with them for a while I realized why he hadn't done the job himself. They had never been shod before and they kept kicking their feet out and leaning on me.

I had a really hard time shoeing those two young horses. I cut my hand on a nail when one of the horses kicked, and I was bleeding a lot. When I looked at my hand and all the blood on it, I remembered a place in the Bible that says, "There is no forgiveness of sin without the shedding of blood."[2] It was then that I knew God wanted me to tell this man about him. So when I finished, the man asked me how much he owed

2. Hebrews 9:22.

Shoeing a pair of tough young horses
in the mountains in Oregon

me for the work I had done. I told him, "No charge."

He couldn't believe that I would work that hard and get cut up in the process for nothing. He asked me why I would do it for free. I told him I did it because I wanted to tell him about Jesus and how he bled and died for him for free because he loved him and wanted to be friends with him. I could tell that what I was saying was making sense, so I asked him if he wanted to ask Jesus into his heart and into his life. He said, "Yes. How do I do it?"

I said, "Pray this prayer with me. Jesus, forgive me of everything I have done wrong, come into my life and help me to serve you."

When we were done praying he gave me a big hug.

It felt like he had never hugged anyone in his whole life because he didn't want to let go. Big fat tears were running down his face and he just kept thanking me and crying and hugging me. I will never forget that big old burly man with tears running down his face, just standing there like a little kid, all happy, tender, and at peace.

Now, if I would have gotten paid for shoeing those horses, at that time the job would have been worth about seventy dollars. I sure could have used the money, but I knew I wasn't supposed to take any. That man came to know Jesus, so it was all good because I got the eternal treasure out of it. Even still, I kept thinking about the money that I could have had as I rode down out of the mountains.

Just about the time I was thinking about how nice it would be to be able to buy some of the different foods I was wanting, a sheep rancher invited me to stay at his house. He gave me a quick tour of the place and told me how his uncle was Jimmy Doolittle, the man who led the first air attack on Japan during Word War II. He gave me the book his uncle had written and also slipped me seventy dollars as I rode off. I had to laugh, God got me again.

I still had a long way to go and my horse's shoes were worn-out, and I mean really worn-out. Her front shoes had started out a half inch thick and were now only about as thick as a quarter. I had packed an extra pair of perfectly bent shoes for each animal before I left home, and had already used them along the ride in

A pile of worn-out, paper-thin horseshoes

Northern California. Just when I was thinking about how much I needed new horseshoes, a farrier pulled up in his truck and asked me what I was doing.[3] I told him I was riding my horse to Canada and telling people about Jesus. We talked for a while. When he saw how worn-out the shoes on my horses were, he said, "I just pulled some almost brand new shoes off my last customer's horse, and you can have them if you want them."

I said, "Yes, that would be great, thanks." So he

---

3. Farriers specialize in horse hoof care; they know how to trim hooves and put shoes on. The job is kind of like the combination of being a blacksmith and a veterinarian.

handed me a slightly used set. After I thanked him again, he went on his way. Later that day when I went to change the horse's shoes, I saw that the set of shoes he'd given me was already bent perfectly to fit my horse; I couldn't believe it. All I had to do was nail them on.[4]

---

4. Horseshoes need to be bent and shaped to fit each hoof of a horse nearly one hundred percent of the time.

Chapter 12

In Oregon

The Willamette Valley held many of the highlights of my trip. Everything there was green and pretty, and the people seemed different than California people. They were really laid-back, super nice, and they drank an awful lot of coffee. I figure I spent about twenty days riding through Oregon. I stayed with people and ate dinner with them fifteen of those twenty days, and I turned down a lot of offers too.

Those days in Oregon were more relaxed, and I would stop several times a day just to let the horses graze. I would pull my boots off, read my Bible, and take a nap. Everyday was like a dream. I just remember being so peaceful inside and thinking, "I have never been as happy as I am now." I would think to myself, "There is no place I would rather be than where I am now, and nothing I

would rather be doing than what I am doing right now."
I love that feeling. It is the definition of happiness.

I'd left home at harvest time, right at the end of May,
and I rode north about thirty miles a day. Well, spring
travels north at thirty miles a day, so springtime came
with me. I liked eating all the different types of food
along the way, basically whatever was growing in season
at the time. I remember Oregon had the best blackber-
ries ever. Man, I ate a ton of those things.

It rained on me off and on almost everyday during
that part of Oregon, so I was always pulling my poncho
on, then off, then on again to stay dry. One time it was
raining on me as the sun went down and a nice lady
invited me to stay at her house, which was just a one
room shack. I felt a little weird about it, but I needed a
place to keep dry and I didn't really have any options. So
I said yes and she cooked me some great food and got
my clothes dry. I spent some time that evening telling
her about Jesus and praying with her just like I always

did when I stayed with people.

The next day I was headed out of town, and a young couple in a car stopped me and with tears in their eyes told me that the lady I had stayed with in the shack was their sister. They were pastors in town and had tried so many times to tell her about Jesus, but she wouldn't listen. They said when I told her about Jesus she believed in him and knew that he was real. They couldn't stop thanking me. They offered me money and anything I needed but I said that them stopping and thanking me was plenty good enough.

On a Saturday, I rode by an old country Presbyterian church; the men of the church were there having a work day. The lead man came up to me with a big chaw of tobacco in his gum and asked me what I was doing. When I told him, he got all excited and insisted that I stay with him. He treated me like a king and took me out shooting and whitewater canoeing. He and his wife took me to church and showed me off to all their friends. I'll always remember that man, how honored he was that I would stay with them, and how much he appreciated what I was doing. He cried when I left.[1]

---

1. I had never seen so many men feel emotion like the men I met on this trip did. A lot of them wanted to come with me, but couldn't because of work or for some other reason. I think part of what moved them was that I was doing something that they had in their hearts to do. Even though they couldn't come, when they helped me they got the chance to connect to the adventure and freedom, and to feel the pleasure of the Lord that they'd had inside of them all along.

Riding up to the church work day and
whitewater canoeing on my way through Oregon

One time I rode into a park and of course there were kids playing there, so I started giving them rides on my horse. After doing that for a while, I started telling the kids why I was riding my horse to Canada and began telling them about Jesus. When I asked if any of them wanted to ask Jesus into their hearts, a bunch of them said yes, so we all prayed together. It was awesome!

Chapter 13

Riding the Mule

By the time I got to Salem my horse had gotten pretty skinny and I was having to stop so much to feed her that I wasn't going very fast at all. I decided to leave her behind and just ride the mule instead. I left my horse with a lady who offered to keep her for a while, and made a plan to pick her up on my way home.

I was down to next to nothing and riding a mule. I didn't think it would be that big a deal, but I had to swallow some pride when I started riding that mule. Sure, the mule was faster, smarter, and a smoother ride, but it just didn't look nearly as cool as the whole Marlboro Man setup I had going on with the horse. I rode on and was a better man for it, even if I didn't look as good.

By the time I made it to Portland, my pants had

Crossing the Columbia River into Washington
over the East Portland Freeway bike
lane with my guide and his bicycle

gotten a lot tighter; I was gaining weight back after not
eating for a while before I left. As I neared the edge of
the city, I got a little worried. I knew that Portland was
big and that I was going to have to ride right through
the busy traffic of the city to get to one of the bridges
that crossed over the Columbia River into Washington.
I wasn't sure what I was going to do.

That night, right on the edge of Portland, I stayed
with a Mexican family who loved Jesus and had tons of
God stories. They treated me like royalty and washed
my clothes by hand. Their young son said he would lead

me through the city on his bike and show me the way across the river. All the next day I followed my guide down a bike trail right through the heart of Portland and across a bridge with the freeway running on both sides of us. I thanked that young boy and gave him a hug. He started crying when we said good-bye.

Chapter 14

Washington

I had seen God do so many amazing things along the way that I really wanted to push it a little further. I decided that when I crossed the Washington border I would take no more than I needed for one day at a time, just to see God provide for me everyday.[1] So, I gave away what money I had and got rid of all my stuff except the clothes I was wearing, my Bible, toothbrush, extra socks and underwear, a pot, a fork, and my sleeping bag.

The mule was a lot faster than my horse, so it seemed like I just blew right through Washington because I didn't have to set up camp anymore or pack up all of that stuff.

---

1. In Exodus 16, the Israelites were only supposed to collect enough manna to feed their families for one day.

Joking around on the way to Washington

For the most part I slept out in hay barns or out in the open under the stars, using the mule's saddle blankets for a bed. I left my tent with my horse in Salem, so if it was raining in Washington, I'd just find something to crawl under to stay dry at night. I didn't even bother to cook my oatmeal most of the time. In the mornings, I'd wake up, put on my hat, brush my teeth, and ride.

In Southern Washington I rode into a big Christian concert and was an attraction for a bit, but I didn't like the attention so I kept riding.

I did stay a few nights with families I met along the way. One family I stayed with had a son who couldn't speak. He would communicate by blinking his eyes and he later wrote me a letter. I stayed with another great family up in Acme, Washington. They were musicians

The Family I stayed with in Acme, Washington

and were shooting a music video that day. I drove into Bellingham Bay with them before dinner and helped with the shoot. That was one of the few times I rode in a car the whole trip. It felt weird.

All those rains in Oregon had turned my hat into a floppy, saggy mess of straw and somewhere along the way, the heel of one of my boots popped off.[2] I found a nail and hammered it back on. It wasn't a problem. I knew I had what I needed and that I'd be fine.

As I neared the Canadian border, I started getting a bit sad that my trip was almost over. I didn't want it to

---

2. After the trip my friend Jon said, "When you got back and I saw your hat, I didn't even need to ask about the trip. Your hat told the whole story."

The family I stayed with in Lynden, Washington

end, but wanted to get there all at the same time. When I rode into Lynden, Washington it was a bright sunny day. I rode my mule right through town, with people feeding me along the way, thinking to myself, "I love this town."[3]

The border was only five miles away. I had made it. The whole way through Washington I never kept any more than I needed for that day; God always gave me

---

3. I didn't know it at the time, but a few years later I would move to Lynden with my new bride, Diane. We started out living in a great little studio just off Main Street. In the first three years we had five different jobs between us, then we started a business, built a home, and had three of our children there. We lived there for a total of twelve years.

what I needed and I never missed a thing.

Those final miles riding north out of Lynden were perfect. The last little bit was flat farmland; bright green hay fields, silage corn, and neat, clean dairies filled the landscape. The mood was upbeat, and the air smelled like home. I could see the Canadian Coastal Mountain Range to the north, the North Cascades to the east, and about fifteen miles west I could see the San Juan Islands popping up out of the ocean in the distance. When I got to the border, I'm not sure what I expected, maybe fireworks or something, but I just walked the mule across the line and that was it.

Chapter 15

Across the Border and Back Again

I took the mule about ten feet across the border, then turned around and rode back into town. I felt a change come over me. I knew my trip was finished and that I was headed back into the real world. There are moments of clarity in life when you see things for what they are; this was one of those times. I was fully present and deeply grateful.

That night I stayed with a family in Lynden who found a place to keep the mule and helped me get a ride back to the Canadian border the next day.[1] I spent the little

---

1. I stayed with the Gerbrandt family, pictured in the previous chapter. Caleb, the little boy in the saddle in the photo, has become a close family friend and has grown into an exceptional man who loves Jesus and has an excellent work ethic. He is always fun to be with.

money I had on food, threw my saddlebag over my shoulder, and started hitchhiking to Alaska.

A lot had changed inside me since I rode out at the beginning of the summer. I had started out with all this stuff, and as the trip went on I carried less and less. I was down to just a few things. I knew what I needed and everything else was unnecessary. I felt light and at the same time strong. I was confident in myself, and in my God. I became reflective and quiet. I would listen more and talk less. I felt fully connected to creation and every time I jumped in a car or truck for a ride it was a bit of a shock to be pulled out of that zone and back into the modern world, moving at seventy miles an hour instead of three.

It felt weird to be on foot and not to have the horses with me. I got passed by hundreds of cars before anyone stopped to pick me up, but I did end up meeting some people who treated me really well and helped me out. One cool surprise was that my cousin Dennis was on his way to do a kayak trip with his family on the Yukon River; he picked me up and I rode with him for a few days.

When I was on my own, I'd camp out by the side of the Alaska Highway at night. Even though it was August, it was really cold at night and I almost froze to death in the Yukon. I made it through the worst night by crawling under a dirty old carpet in an abandoned trailer near the highway.

All in all, it took about eight days to make it to my

Hitchhiking the ALCAN Highway to Alaska

friend Jim's house in Alaska.[2] In just one week I'd covered nearly twice the distance it had taken me the whole summer to ride.

Everything was huge in Alaska, the mountains, the wilderness, all of it. The scale of the landscape made me feel small, but not in a bad way. Once I made it to Jim's, we went fishing everyday. It was good to be with my friend. We spent about a week just sitting by the lake catching fish and smoking salmon.

When the time had come to go back home, I got a

2. I started and ended the trip at Jim's. He had moved to Alaska to be a fishing guide after graduation and still runs a guiding and lodging business near Soldotna, Alaska: www.jimmiejackfishing.com. He regularly sends us a case of salmon and stays with us a week or so in the winter to warm up. I'm really thankful for his friendship over all these years.

plane ticket to Seattle.[3] My older brother Vernon and my nephew Erik drove out with the horse trailer to pick me up at the airport. We went to get the mule then picked up my horse on the way home. She was so happy to see us that she ran around like crazy for a long time. The mule was really happy to see her too.

The next day as we were driving along, the truck's transmission caught on fire. It was going to take two days to fix it, so my brother and Erik took a bus home because they had to get back for work. I stayed behind so I could drive the truck home after the repairs had been made.

After the truck was up and running again, I stopped for gas and gave a hitchhiker a ride down the road. We were talking and he asked me what I was doing. I told him a bunch of stories and he got chicken skin all over his body and told me that he wanted to have Jesus in his

---

3. Jim's parents bought my ticket, since I still didn't have any money with me. I mailed them a check to pay them back once I got home.

My friend Jim and I with a bunch of
salmon on the Little Sue River

life and be baptized. Right when he said that we crossed a river. I pulled over and we waded out into the water in the dark in our underwear, and I baptized him right there. Afterward we went into a roadside restaurant to get burgers, still sopping wet. We said good-bye and I kept driving south.

When I got back home I felt really different. I had trouble sitting in chairs and my bed felt like too much of a luxury. I had a hard time getting along with a watch instead of the sun, and had a bit of a hard time relating to people. Even though I knew they loved me, I couldn't really connect very well again.

In the middle of all these feelings and just a few months after I got back home, a bunch of my friends invited me to go to a New Year's Eve party in Anaheim. It was at that party that I met my wife. I knew the second I saw her that I was going to marry her. We danced, and later hung out all night until the sun came up. I didn't sleep or eat for three days after that, I just couldn't. When I couldn't take it anymore I called my friend Brian to come over and pray for me.[4] When he did, I finally fell asleep and slept for twenty hours straight.

---

4. Brian Falls has been my Jesus Freak friend for over twenty years. I love this guy and I can't say enough about him. He's the real deal.

***

My horse trip affected the lives of a lot of people along the way and over the years, especially me.[5] Sometimes I think about it and smile when I remember what God did through me and in me over those fifteen hundred miles. The big lesson I learned is that I don't have to have everything worked out, and I don't have to do it all myself. He is there to help me all the time and in every way. Sometimes when I get worried about money, I remember what God did for me, and I remind myself that it was me who rode my horse to Canada with no food or money without missing one meal.[6]

---

5. One story that I am most proud of is that of my friend Jaime Gilentine. He and I rode motorcycles ten thousand miles from Yorba Linda, California to Santiago, Chile before I flew to New Zealand to marry Diane. A decade after my trip, Jaime was going to seminary in Maine. One day his professor had each of the students stand up and tell the most important moment they'd ever had in their spiritual lives. As they went around the room, a woman from Oregon stood up and said, "Ten years ago, a man on a horse came riding through our town telling people about Jesus. I will never forget him for the rest of my life because you could see Jesus in him and you could feel him too, and that impacted my faith in God more than anything else in my life."

6. Luke 22:35.

ABOUT THE AUTHOR

Mark Peterson lives in Northern California with his wife, Diane, and their four kids, Levi, Clay, Joy, and Jubilee. *Man on a Horse* is his first book.

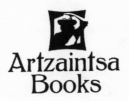

Artzaintsa
Books

Made in the USA
San Bernardino, CA
30 January 2014